ESSENTIAL TIPS

101

RELAXATION

ESSENTIAL TIPS
101

RELAXATION

Nitya Lacroix

DK PUBLISHING, INC.

A DK PUBLISHING BOOK

Editor Damien Moore
Art Editor Roger Daniels
Senior Editor Gillian Roberts
Series Art Editor Alison Donovan
Production Controller Jenny May
US Editor Ray Rogers

First American Edition, 1998
2 4 6 8 10 9 7 5 3 1
Published in the United States by DK Publishing, Inc.
95 Madison Avenue, New York, New York 10016

Visit us on the World Wide Web at http://www.dk.com

ISBN 0-7894-2775-3

Text film output by R&B Creative Services Ltd, Great Britain
Reproduced by Colourscan, Singapore
Printed and bound in Italy by Graphicom

ESSENTIAL TIPS

WHAT IS RELAXATION?

1 WHY RELAXATION IS NECESSARY

Learning how to relax will enhance your quality of life by counteracting the negative effects of stress. By taking the time to relax properly, you are able to release accumulated mental and physical tension, thus restoring depleted energy levels. This leaves you feeling refreshed, revitalized, and better able to cope with the many pressures of modern living. Relaxation returns you to a sense of wholeness and well-being.

ACTIVE RELAXATION
Leisure sports can help balance the unwanted effects of mental stress (Tip 79).

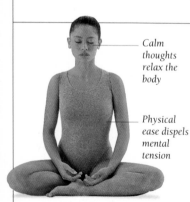

Calm thoughts relax the body

Physical ease dispels mental tension

TAKE TIME TO RELAX

2 HOW RELAXATION AFFECTS MIND & BODY

A great many medical experts now acknowledge that body and mind are integrally linked, and that the state of one affects the well-being of the other. Stress lowers the resistance of the body's immune system, whereas a relaxed mind helps strengthen your defense system against disease. In a similar way, when you feel physically relaxed, you will be mentally more at peace.

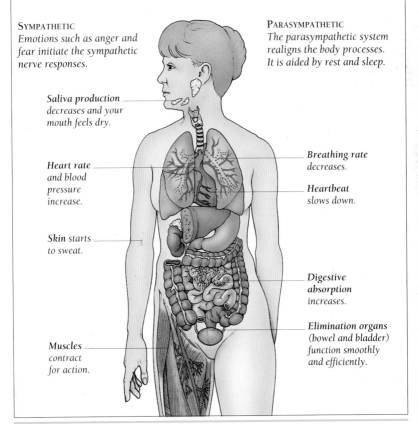
3 THE AUTONOMIC NERVOUS SYSTEM

The autonomic nervous system governs your involuntary responses to stress factors, while enabling your physiological system to return to a state of relaxation once the stressful event has passed. It is divided into two parts, the sympathetic nerves and the parasympathetic nerves, both of which supply most of the major organs of the body. The sympathetic nervous system initiates dramatic physical changes in your body through its "fight or flight" response to stressful stimuli. The parasympathetic nerves help redress these changes, enabling the body to discharge tension and restoring equilibrium to the whole system.

SYMPATHETIC
Emotions such as anger and fear initiate the sympathetic nerve responses.

PARASYMPATHETIC
The parasympathetic system realigns the body processes. It is aided by rest and sleep.

Saliva production *decreases and your mouth feels dry.*

Heart rate *and blood pressure increase.*

Skin *starts to sweat.*

Muscles *contract for action.*

Breathing rate *decreases.*

Heartbeat *slows down.*

Digestive absorption *increases.*

Elimination organs *(bowel and bladder) function smoothly and efficiently.*

9

4 BODY AWARENESS

Learn to recognize areas of physical tension so you can start to relax them. Stand up, close your eyes, and focus your attention on each body part. Ask yourself: Is this area contracted or relaxed? Is it balanced or under strain? Are your knees flexible? Do your feet feel secure and rooted to the ground?

Are your jaw and mouth relaxed or rigid?

Are your head and neck in line with the rest of your spine, or is your head tilted?

Are you breathing fully, using your diaphragm?

Does your breath sink down into your abdomen?

Do your hands feel loose and relaxed, or are your fingers clenched?

Are your knees flexible, or locked and tense?

Do your calves and ankles feel relaxed?

FOCUSING YOUR BREATH
As you focus on each body part, consciously send your breath toward it and let it become relaxed and loose.

5 MIND AWARENESS

Knowing and understanding your strengths and weaknesses will equip you with the awareness to change your life in positive ways. Even if you feel confident and relaxed about most aspects of your life, be honest with yourself about those areas where you feel stressed. Take time to appraise your feelings regularly.

MAKE A LIST
Write out a list of positive and negative influences in your life. Aim to change the stressful factors to areas of satisfaction.

6 ARE YOU ABLE TO RELAX?

The following eight questions may help you to pinpoint those areas of your life where you are experiencing stress. If you answer "yes" to any of the questions, then you will benefit from the relaxation techniques that are described in this book. Unlocking the tension in any one area will bring a multitude of benefits for your whole life.

DOES YOUR BODY FEEL TENSE?
General discomfort and pain in the body are often the result of both physical and mental stress, caused by harmful postural habits or inhibited emotions, such as fear or anger. Breathing exercises, postural awareness, and massage therapy release tension from both body and mind.

DO YOU SUFFER FROM PANIC ATTACKS?
Chronic anxiety and panic attacks are very debilitating. Look for the underlying causes of stress in your life and seek to remedy them. Learn breathing techniques to help reduce anxiety.

DO YOU FIND IT HARD TO HAVE FUN?
Do you have difficulty relaxing and enjoying yourself? Taking up a sociable sport encourages you to enjoy the company of others. Physical activity releases tension.

DO YOU LACK DRIVE AND MOTIVATION?
Inertia often has its origins in a medical condition such as depression: in this case, seek your doctor's advice. However, it may be linked to dissatisfaction about certain circumstances in your life. Identify what is draining your energy, and take steps to make changes where appropriate.

ARE YOU TOO BUSY TO EAT HEALTHILY?
A basic rule of health is to eat regular, nutritious meals. However, it is usually the first rule to be abandoned when you most need it – during periods of stress. Resolve to stick to a healthy diet – no matter how busy you are – to keep your blood-sugar and energy levels steady.

DO YOU FIND IT HARD TO RELATE TO OTHERS?
Build your confidence by nurturing relationships that make you feel good about yourself. Be sure to communicate your needs clearly.

DO YOU TAKE ON TOO MUCH WORK?
Don't allow your work to dominate your life. Spend quality time with your family and friends, and develop a healthy balance between work and leisure.

ARE YOUR THOUGHTS MOSTLY NEGATIVE?
Do you feel envious of others? Do you think that life is passing you by? Do you always imagine the worst? If so, you need to change the subconscious thoughts that negatively govern your life. Affirmations, positive thinking, and visualizations can help you rethink your attitudes.

BODY EASE & STRETCHING

7 MIND–BODY CONNECTION

Relaxation is the key to unlock the physical tension that forms as protection against emotional stress. This type of tension tends to root itself between the major body parts, creating tight bands of muscle that cause one area of the body to feel "cut off" from another. Breathing into and relaxing chronically tense areas of your body will help you to identify and release any underlying stress. The term "carrying the world on your shoulders" aptly describes the mind–body connection.

The set of your shoulders indicates your mental state

Face muscles *tighten under stress to present an acceptable public mask.*

WHAT LIES BENEATH?
Individual parts of the body respond to different kinds of stress, so you can use your body to chart your mental health.

Knees *reflect your attitudes toward control and weakness.*

Back muscles *form a protective shield against stress.*

The pelvis *is linked to feelings concerning survival and pleasure.*

Legs *relate to childhood emotions like rage.*

8 EXPELLING TENSION

Return a sense of ease to your body and mind by using this exercise to release any pent-up emotions and muscular tightness.

Lie down on your back on a firm, flat surface and focus attention on each part of your body individually, moving from your toes up toward your face. Release the tension in one area at a time by simply contracting the appropriate muscles, and then let go. First, contract your muscles as you inhale. Next, hold your breath until you feel that you must exhale: then, relax the area as you do so.

• Make a sound to express the release as you exhale and relax the area you are working on.
• Become aware of the increased vitality of the body part that you have just relaxed.

▷ **BRISK ACTIVITY**
Jogging or taking a brisk walk after work will help you to release any tension accumulated during the day.

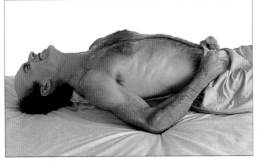

TIGHTEN & RELEASE
To finish off the exercise above, tighten and then release your entire body. Rest for ten minutes afterward.

KNOW YOUR BODY
Be aware of your body's reaction to stress, so you can quickly dispel tension.

---

9 BODY LANGUAGE

Your body constantly reflects what you are feeling, even if you are overtly intending to give a different impression. Become alert to your body language, and develop a more relaxed posture so you can project a less defensive stance when you communicate with people.

BE OPEN
Uncross your arms and make eye contact to show that you are friendly and open.

10 CORRECT POSTURAL ALIGNMENT

The postural ease of certain parts of the body is essential to its correct structural alignment and its ability to function easily and with grace. Postural imbalance is invariably due to trauma, chronic muscular tension, or the way that you habitually sit and move. You can regain healthy postural balance by taking a course of lessons from a qualified postural technique teacher. Chronic tension can be alleviated by deep tissue massage and other forms of body therapy. You can unlock harmful postural habits by bringing a new awareness to important areas such as your head, neck, and spine.

Head and neck in line with rest of spine

Jaw relaxes

Arms lengthen down

Knees loosen

Feet solidly connect with ground

BALANCED BODY
A balanced structural alignment will increase your sense of ease with your body.

11 RELEASING POSTURAL TENSION

Visualization (*Tip 50*)can release postural tension. Think of your head as a balloon floating up toward the sky, causing your neck to extend up from your shoulders and your spine to lengthen. As your upper body lifts up gracefully against the pull of gravity, your lower body provides a stable connection with the earth.

FLOATING BALLOON

12 SITTING COMFORTABLY

Check your posture to see if you are sitting correctly, especially when your intention is to relax. It is very easy to relapse into awkward positions when you get engrossed in conversation, or are concentrating at work, or just watching television. Doing so will diminish the depth of your breathing and strain your joints and muscles. Do your best to adopt and maintain an open, balanced posture when sitting.

◁ BAD HABITS
Sitting cross-legged for long periods can cause lower back problems. Hunching your shoulders or slumping adds stress to your spine.

▷ RELAXED POSITION
Sit so that you can breathe fully. Keep your pelvis balanced to help lengthen and relax your spine.

13 Sitting for Long Periods

Arrange your seat and equipment for maximum comfort whenever your work requires you to spend long periods sitting at a desk. Keep your head balanced and your spine extended. Adjust the height of your chair so that your hips are slightly higher than your knees.

MOVE AROUND
A foot rest aids circulation, as does flexing your feet and leg muscles. Take breaks to stretch your spine and ease your shoulders.

14 Standing for Long Periods

If you stand for long periods during work hours, don't strain your spine by leaning heavily on one hip or the other to rest your legs. Move around to boost your circulation, and have a chair at hand so you can sit when the opportunity arises.

FOOTSTOOL
A footstool allows you to take the weight off one leg at a time without straining your spine. It helps to relax your ankles and knees while keeping your posture in balance.

Change feet every few minutes

15 LYING DOWN COMFORTABLY

Most people suffer at one time or another from back pain, which robs business and industry worldwide of many working days each year. Occasionally, chronic structural misalignment will be the cause; however, the discomfort of this common ailment is usually temporary. The upper and lower back and neck are the most likely sites of pain in the spine. If you are experiencing back problems (and especially if they recur), take every opportunity to lie down and rest your spine to relieve it from the pull of gravity and its function of supporting your body.

Placing a small cushion, pillow, or rolled towel under your neck or lower back can help release tension and alleviate pain in these key areas, and free your spine from stress.

LOWER BACK
Take the strain off your lower back by lying down on a supportive surface. Relax each part of your body, releasing your weight into the ground.

Place pillow under lower back

Pillow under knees releases tension in pelvic region

LENGTHEN THE SPINE
This position helps to lengthen the spine and releases tension around tight vertebrae.

Raise knees to ease hip joints

Cushion helps to extend neck comfortably

Place hands on abdomen and breathe deeply

Place feet flat on ground

16 WALKING

Allow your movements to become fluid and graceful when you are walking. Imagining that you have a heavy "tail" sinking down to the earth will encourage you to drop the weight of your pelvis, buttocks, and legs toward the ground. At the same time, visualize your upper body, spine (your neck is part of your spine), and head lengthening upward and becoming very light.

STEPS TO GOOD HEALTH
A brisk walk provides excellent cardiovascular exercise. It helps strengthen the bones without putting strain on your spine.

THINK WIDE
Let your arms swing loosely at your sides, and feel the sense of space within your chest and shoulders. Breathe deeply.

17 EASING TIRED LEGS

Bring relief to tired, aching legs and feet by lying down flat on your back for 10–20 minutes and raising your lower limbs above your heart level. This simple exercise assists the blood flow from your extremities back toward the heart and boosts the drainage of a sluggish lymph system, which can cause the legs and feet to swell when you have been standing for long periods.

RAISED LEGS
Use a chair to raise your legs and feet while ensuring your knees are relaxed. Rub cooling peppermint foot lotion into aching feet.

18 HOLDING OBJECTS

Try to undo harmful postural habits that can create physical stress while you are performing everyday tasks, such as holding a phone or a pen. Become aware of your tension patterns by noticing the tightness of your grip, whether you are tensing your jaw, or if you are holding your breath. Consciously relax and adopt a looser, more comfortable posture.

Relax your grip on the phone

CONSERVE ENERGY
There is no need to involve your whole body just to perform a single simple task. Save energy by isolating your movement to the specific body part that needs to be employed to complete a task.

19 AVOID HAND STRAIN

Both at home and at work, regard your hands as vital tools and keep them supple and dextrous. Regular hand exercises decrease the risk of developing stiff joints and tendons, which can occur through repetitive actions. Stimulate the nerve endings, increase the flexibility, and improve the coordination of your hands by squeezing rubbery objects, such as juggling balls or modeling clay.

SHOU XING
These silver balls, called Shou Xing by the Chinese, are employed in Oriental healing practice to keep hands supple.

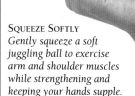

SQUEEZE SOFTLY
Gently squeeze a soft juggling ball to exercise arm and shoulder muscles while strengthening and keeping your hands supple.

20 STRETCHING TO RELAX

Stretch like a cat to relax, limber, and tone your whole body. Join a stretch or yoga class to learn the correct application of postures to extend and flex your body, then try to practice every day at home.

Stretching and yoga are holistic therapies benefiting both the body and mind. Remember to breathe fully into each movement. If in doubt, check with your doctor before attempting this exercise.

1 Lie flat on your stomach, with your hands placed next to your shoulders. Lever yourself into the kneeling posture, moving your arms forward, then lower your forehead to the ground.

Feel the stretch in your back and arms

Tones buttocks and thighs

2 While still kneeling, slide your hands directly below your shoulders. Lower you head, and draw your right knee up toward it to extend your back muscles.

Knee flexes toward head

Keep leg straight

Lengthen spine

3 Now extend your right leg behind you, raising it as high as possible. At the same time, lift your head. Repeat with the left leg.

21 SHOULDERS & NECK RELEASE

Keep wrist (and elbow joint) loose

Keeping your shoulders and neck flexible will do wonders for your whole posture. By loosening these muscles, you increase the healthy flow of blood to your brain (muscular tension can inhibit it). Use both of these stretches in the morning – after taking a shower to warm and relax the area – so you can start the day feeling more alert. Releasing constriction from your neck and shoulders will also free you from tiredness and strain after an extended period of work or study.

EASY STRETCH
Using the top vertebrae of your spine as a pivotal point, rotate your head slowly five times to the left, and then five times to the right, to bring an easy stretch in your neck.

BE GENTLE
Perform these exercises slowly and gently to avoid causing any trauma to the neck and shoulder joints. Make each movement the focus of your complete attention.

CIRCULAR STRETCH
Make five circles with one arm at a time, raising it up and behind your head before lowering. Repeat in the opposite direction.

21

22 RELEASE TENSION IN YOUR SPINE

Your spine is your body's main support system, and its flexibility is fundamental to your sense of well-being and ease of movement. The spinal column houses your central nervous system, which serves your whole body. Releasing tension in your spine and exercising your back increases your vitality and improves your posture. The movements described here help you gently stretch and flex your spine.

1 ◁ Place your feet shoulder-width apart, flex your knees slightly, then stretch your whole body upward to the tips of your outstretched fingers.

Head flops forward

Keep feet flat on ground

Hands hang loosely

SPINE CARE
Firming and toning your abdominal muscles will increase support for your back and spine.

2 △ Flop gently forward, with your head held loosely and leading the movement, so that your spine is relaxed and your fingers brush the ground.

3 △ Slowly and gradually uncurl your spine, so that your neck and head are the last areas to come back up into the original standing position.

23 STRETCH TO EASE LOWER BACK PAIN

Curling up takes the pressure off your spine and can ease lower back pain. Lie down and draw both knees up toward your chest, clasping them with your hands. Lift your head forward to meet them, and hold the position for 10 seconds. Then gently return to lying flat on the ground, with your arms and legs outstretched, to relax completely.

BACK CURL CAN GIVE RELIEF

24 ENCOURAGE VITALITY

Many leisure pursuits increase your body's vitality and fitness, so aiding relaxation. Swimming tones and relaxes your whole body, while dancing is one of the best work-outs you can do – it's an excellent tonic for your spirits, too.

LET GO
Dancing freely and joyfully enables you to let go of physical and mental tension.

WATER THERAPY
Swimming is often recommended as a therapy for people with back problems.

BREATH AWARENESS

25 BREATHING & RELAXATION

Deep, slow, steady breathing relaxes your entire body and calms your mind. As you inhale, oxygen is brought into your bloodstream, energizing every cell in your body; then, as you exhale, toxic wastes are expelled. Breathing in this way increases your physical vitality and energy while creating mental and emotional balance.

Let your thoughts fade away

MEDITATIVE MOMENTS
Sit quietly in the morning and evening, and bring your attention to your breathing.

Breathe in and out through your nostrils

Keep your chest open and wide

Let your breath fill your lungs

Diaphragm rises and falls as you breathe

Relax your hands, arms, and shoulders

26 STEADYING THE BREATHING RHYTHM

Focusing on and steadying the rhythm of your breath initiates highly relaxing psychological and physiological changes. Techniques of breath awareness are crucial to the ancient practice of meditation, which is used to enhance clarity of consciousness by stilling the mind. Nowadays, many medical experts acknowledge that these practices are advantageous for the health of the whole body. By breathing fully and steadily, and concentrating on the breath for specific periods of time, you can calm the nervous system, slow down the heartbeat, and cause changes in the pattern of your brain waves that soothe your entire being.

- Keep your eyes closed and breathe in and out through your nose.
- Practice initially for 15 minutes daily, increasing up to 40 minutes.
- Rest for five minutes after practice.

◁ REMAIN FOCUSED
Keep your attention focused on the rise and fall of your diaphragm as you inhale and exhale. Breathe into your stomach, not your chest.

▷ EXHALE FULLY
Place greater emphasis on your exhalation to expel air from your lungs, and your inhalation will naturally return more deeply.

Sit on a cushion to support your pelvis, or use a straight-backed chair if necessary.

Hands on belly help focus on breathing.

Sit with a straight and relaxed posture; keep your spine fully extended.

27 BREATHING & MOVEMENT

Consciously integrate breathing with movement to still your mind and increase your awareness of the subtleties of your body. For just 15 minutes each day, walk slowly and deliberately. Walk barefoot so that you are able to feel close contact with the ground. Inhale deeply as one leg rises. Feel as if the leg is being lifted up from the knee by a string. Exhale fully as you sink your foot into the ground, rolling the weight from the heel to the ball. Keep your spine straight.

GROUND CONTACT
Feel each step of your feet as they contact the ground, and synchronize your breathing with the slow motion.

28 BREATHING FOR DEEP RELAXATION

Lie down flat on your back with your arms stretched out beside you, then close your eyes and relax into the supportive surface of the ground beneath you. Inhale deeply into your abdomen. As you exhale slowly, feel your whole body weight sinking gradually deeper down into the ground. Breathe deeply and fully for at least five minutes.

CORPSE POSE
In yoga, this position is known as the corpse pose. As you exhale, focus on releasing tension from your shoulders and spine.

Feet roll out naturally

Arms spread out, palms upward, fingers slightly curled

29 BREATHING TO REDUCE ANXIETY

Breathing rhythmically and slowly will help you to cope with feelings of anxiety and will allow you to remain calm during stressful times. Check that you are breathing deeply into your abdomen and that you are using your diaphragm correctly, so that your lungs are fully absorbing oxygen from the air and expelling carbon dioxide. Breathe in to a count of four, and exhale to a count of five. During stressful periods, sit for ten minutes a day, breathing deeply and evenly.

FEEL HOW YOU BREATHE
Sit comfortably on the floor or in a straight-backed chair. Place one hand over your lower ribs to feel the rise and fall of your breath. As you inhale, your chest wall expands outward, and as you exhale, it recoils inward.

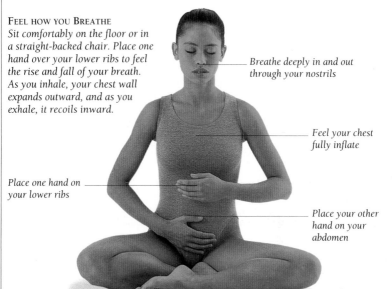

Breathe deeply in and out through your nostrils

Feel your chest fully inflate

Place one hand on your lower ribs

Place your other hand on your abdomen

30 BREATHING DURING A PANIC ATTACK

Panic attacks are frequently brought on by over-breathing, which causes excess carbon dioxide to be expelled. Distressing symptoms such as dizziness, extreme fear, and heart palpitations are experienced. If you are panicky, breathe slowly and deeply (*Tip 29*). If you are feel that you are hyperventilating, breathe in some carbon dioxide by cupping your hands over your mouth and nose. Focus on your body and try to relax your muscles. Reassure yourself that you are in control.

MASSAGE & LOOSENING UP

31 BENEFITS OF MASSAGE

Massage is one of the most beneficial therapies for relaxation. It eases pain and tension out of the body, brings vitality to a sluggish system, soothes an overactive mind, and calms the nervous system. The caring touch of hands on skin can dispel feelings of isolation and alienation, and return a sense of wholeness and well-being to mind and body.

- Massage boosts the circulatory system.
- It releases postural stress.
- Toxic deposits in tissue are eliminated.
- It encourages a healthy body image.

STRESS RELEASE
Massage is the perfect antidote to stress. The more relaxed and receptive you become, the better it feels.

32 CHOOSING A PROFESSIONAL MASSAGE THERAPIST

Treating yourself to a good professional massage for relaxation is money well spent, but it is worth investing a little time to find a reliable therapist. Recommendation by word of mouth is best. Ask for proof of professional qualifications, and be sure to check that the style of massage is appropriate to your needs.

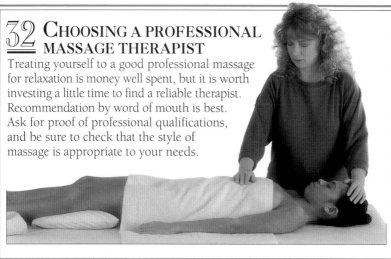

33 MASSAGE WITH A PARTNER

Be aware of your own posture

Relax in the comfort of your home by giving or receiving a massage with a partner or friend. Learn the basic strokes from a massage book, or participate in a workshop, so that you can spontaneously respond to each other in times of need. Remember that even the most basic strokes can feel good if they are applied in a flowing, rhythmical manner.

Let your hands be supple

ENJOY GIVING
Giving a massage can be just as relaxing as receiving one.

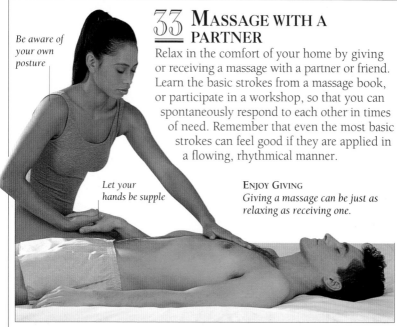

34 AMBIENCE & EQUIPMENT

Set up a welcoming ambience for your massage to enhance its effects. Choose a warm room that provides privacy, and remove all clutter. Lay out your massage equipment neatly, and place a supportive mattress or blankets on the floor. Use sheets to cover both the mattress and your partner, and have cushions and pillows handy for added comfort. Soft lighting adds to the ambience.

WARM ROOM
Ensure that the room is warm and draft free, but ventilated to keep the air fresh. An open fire creates the perfect ambience.

◁ **MASSAGE COUCH**
If massaging on the floor is uncomfortable for you, a portable fold-away massage couch is ideal.

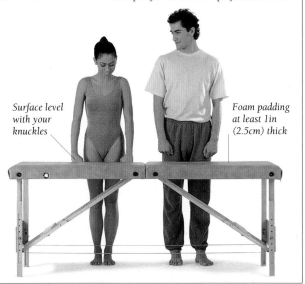

Surface level with your knuckles

Foam padding at least 1in (2.5cm) thick

STURDY COUCH
A massage couch should be at least 6ft (1.8m) long, and about 2–2½ft (0.8m) wide.

35 AROMATHERAPY & MASSAGE OILS

Aromatherapy is becoming increasingly popular as a healing art, and it can be combined with massage to induce a state of deep relaxation. Aromatic essential oils are extracted from flowers, herbs, and resins. Precise dosages of these essences can be combined with vegetable oils to create a suitable lubricant for massage strokes.

KEEP ESSENTIAL OILS TIGHTLY STOPPERED

36 OILS TO UNWIND & RELAX

A combination of essential oils that both revitalize and calm the senses is perfect for a relaxing massage. Essential oils are highly concentrated, so be sure to create recipes using the correct amount of drops combined with a pure vegetable oil such as grapeseed, sunflower, or almond. Here is one recipe for a whole body massage: 7 drops of benzoin to warm and energize the body, combined with 7 drops of lavender for calming effects and 4 drops of chamomile to soothe the skin. Dilute these essential oils by mixing them into 1fl oz (30ml) of pure vegetable oil.

RELAXING BLENDS

31

37 BACK MASSAGE

Treat your partner to a relaxing back massage. Spread oil over the whole surface of the back and start with soft, flowing, and rounded movements to relax and warm the tissues and increase circulation. Then focus on the key areas of tension, such as along the spine, lower back, and shoulders. Use your thumbs, fingers, and the heels of your hands to gently manipulate the muscles. The instructions given here show three stages of one long stroke that can be used to begin and end a back massage.

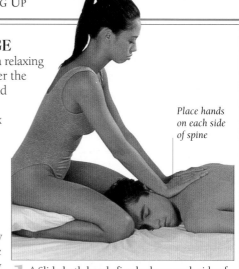

Place hands on each side of spine

1 △ Slide both hands firmly down each side of the spine before fanning them out at the base of the ribcage to the sides of the body.

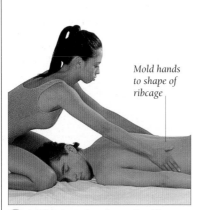

Mold hands to shape of ribcage

2 △ Glide your hands up the sides of the back, swinging them in and around the shoulder blades and firmly back out over the tops of the shoulders.

Sweep hands lightly out over head

3 △ Flex your wrists so your hands glide around the shoulder joints, then draw them lightly back over the shoulders and along the back of the neck.

38 FACE MASSAGE

Pamper your partner with a facial massage to remove the stress of the day. Ensure that your touch is sensitive in this vulnerable area and that your strokes are steady and firm. Follow the contours of your partner's face with your fingers. Start by molding your hands gently around the crown of the head for several moments. Then rub a little oil onto your palms.

1 △ Draw your thumbs from the center of the brow outward, then make small circular strokes at the temples. Repeat over the whole forehead.

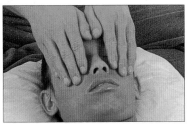

2 △ Rub your hands together briskly to generate heat, then place them gently over the eyes. Softly stroke around the eye sockets with your fingertips.

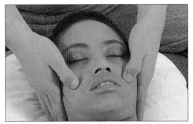

3 △ Glide your thumbpads down the sides of the nose and into the muscle directly under the cheekbones, drawing the thumbs out to the sides of the head.

4 △ Rotate your fingertips over the fleshy area of the cheeks and then knead the chin and jawline with short, alternating strokes from your thumbs.

5 △ Sweeping caresses from the palms of your hands will relax the jaw and mouth. Tenderly stroke up each side of the face, using alternating hands.

39 FOOT MASSAGE

A foot massage benefits the whole body by removing strain from an area that supports its structure and weight. By manipulating and stroking the feet, you encourage greater suppleness in their complex network of bones, tendons, and ligaments. In addition, foot massage stimulates the thousands of nerve endings located in the soles – and is a deeply relaxing experience.

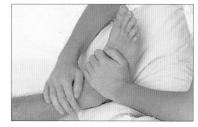

1 △ Warm the foot by stroking lotion from the toes to the ankle. Fan your hands out around the ankle, gliding your fingers gently back along the sole.

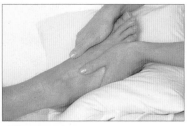

2 △ Stretch the foot by pressing your fingers against the sole while sliding your thumbs out toward the edges. Work up in stages to the ankle.

3 △ The heel of your palm fits perfectly into the contours of the foot, so use it to make firm circular strokes all over the sole, sides, arches, and instep.

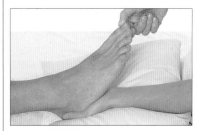

4 △ Support the heel of the foot with one hand, and use the thumb and index finger of the other hand to pull gently along each toe from base to tip.

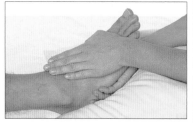

5 △ Cradle the foot between your hands to finish and to create a calming effect by drawing energy down the body. Repeat Steps 1–5 on the other foot.

40 SELF-MASSAGE

Massaging your own body can ease stiffness in tense muscles in addition to invigorating your blood circulation and revitalizing your system. Soothing strokes warm your muscles and stimulate nerve endings. Brisk percussion strokes, such as hacking and pummelling, boost your blood flow, breaking down toxic deposits and relieving tight spots.

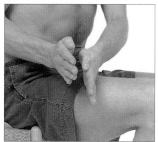

BRISK HACKING MOVEMENT

41 MASSAGE YOUR HEAD, NECK, & SHOULDERS

A self-massage on your head, neck, and shoulders is a stimulating way to start your day. It will clear your mind, increase the circulation to your brain, and alleviate tension from the important postural areas of your shoulders and neck. Focus on invigorating and vibratory strokes, such as hacking, tapping, and pummelling, for maximum boost to your energy levels.

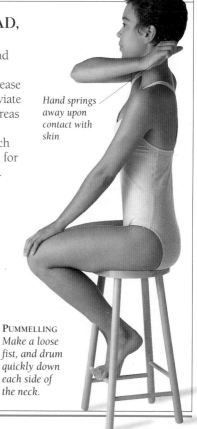

Hand springs away upon contact with skin

TAPPING HEAD
With wrists loose, tap your fingers quickly and rhythmically over your scalp, moving from front to back, then down the sides.

PUMMELLING
Make a loose fist, and drum quickly down each side of the neck.

42 MASSAGE YOUR HANDS

Regularly massage your hands so that they remain supple and free of tension, especially if your work requires repetitive hand movement. Use the fingers, thumb, and heel of one hand to stroke and stretch the muscles, tendons, and bones of the other hand.

FIRM PRESSURE
Rotate your wrist gently and wiggle your fingers. Press all over the palm with small rotary motions of the thumbpad.

PRESS & PULL
Press your thumb over the back of the hand. Stretch along each finger from base to tip with your other thumb and forefinger.

STRETCH OUT
To relieve cramped hands, place them, palm to palm, with your fingers pointing up. Raise your elbows until your palms separate and your fingers press together.

Elbows positioned at right angles to body

Place foot on opposite thigh

43 MASSAGE YOUR FEET & LEGS

Self-massage on the feet is a quick remedy for whole-body relaxation. Soak your feet for ten minutes in warm water with added herbal salts. Dry each foot by wrapping it in a towel and gently squeezing all over. Press your calf muscles to remove stiffness, then rotate your ankle five times in each direction. Stroke, squeeze, and stretch your foot and toes with your palms, fingers, and thumbs to ease out tension.

1 ◁ Using a press-release motion, massage all over your sole. Apply a constant, firm pressure.

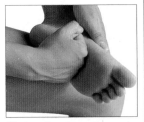

2 △ Make a loose fist, and then firmly slide your knuckles at a steady stretch from the edge of the heel to the base of the toes.

44 SHAKE OUT TENSION

After a relaxing self-massage, shake out any remaining tension. This frees up tight areas and enlivens you by bringing movement to your whole body. Start the shaking from your feet: let the motion travel upward and gradually increase in intensity. Do not force movement. Let every part tremble and shake, particularly inflexible spots such as the shoulders, neck, and head. When you have finished the exercise, relax quietly for a period of at least ten minutes.

THINKING POSITIVELY

45 MIND OVER MATTER

Your mind is a powerful tool: use it to overcome obstacles that are standing in your way so that you can expand your horizons. Have faith in your own abilities, and refuse to accept conditioned beliefs that limit your aspirations. Set your mind firmly on your goals, and strive to fulfill your ambitions.

FEEL EMPOWERED
You don't need to be limited by gender, age, or circumstance. Aim to master the necessary skills to achieve your goals.

46 PERSPECTIVE & ATTITUDE

Examine your attitude to life, and change negative perspectives to positive ones. Instead of being envious of other people, consider what is unique and special in your own life and be happy for other people's success. Counteract each pessimistic thought with an optimistic one, and try to acknowledge and feel grateful for what you have, using that as a basis for enthusiasm about your future. Greet every new day as a fresh beginning.

Is the glass half full or half empty?

47 THE POWER OF AFFIRMATIONS

You have the ability to change your subconscious thoughts with positive affirmations, and so create the life you want. Conscious positive thoughts, such as "I am worthy of love" or "I can succeed in my work," can be accepted by your subconscious and soon replace negative beliefs that exert a hidden but potent influence over you. Look at your reflection in the mirror each morning as you make affirmations for the day: you will soon notice the difference in your demeanor.

BELIEVE IN YOURSELF
Think positively. Affirm each morning that you are worthy of achieving success, love, contentment, and respect.

48 CULTIVATE A SENSE OF HUMOR

Laughter is contagious! Smile at people, and when they smile back, you will feel even better. Think of something humorous, and your worries lighten. Sharing your sense of fun is therapeutic for everyone.

49 USE BOTH SIDES OF YOUR BRAIN

Your brain has two hemispheres. The left hemisphere, the dominant area, controls the right side of the body. It is in charge of functions such as speech, writing, logical thinking, and abstract conception. The right hemisphere controls the left side of the body. It is associated with creativity, spatial relationships, and intuition. Drawing or listening to music enhances right-hemisphere activity, while thought-provoking games such as crossword puzzles stimulate the left side. Relaxation techniques such as meditation encourage both sides of your brain to work in harmony together.

50 WHAT IS VISUALIZATION?

Visualization is a self-help technique that uses positive imagery to effect a desired change in body, mind, or personal circumstances. It is used in numerous forms of therapy and meditation, including hypnosis. It is claimed to aid relaxation, to heal sickness and injuries, to overcome anxiety and phobias, to improve memory, to help increase spiritual consciousness, and to encourage a higher level of self-esteem.

BEAUTIFUL SETTING
Imagining yourself walking on a beautiful beach at sunset, or listening to the lap of the waves, can produce feelings of calm.

51 USING VISUALIZATION

To be effective, visualization therapy requires deep concentration and regular practice. Sit down in a quiet room for 15 minutes. For the first five minutes breathe deeply and relax your body. Form the intention of your visualization, and use your imagination to create a picture of what you wish to accomplish. For example, if you are experiencing pain, imagine a golden light being drawn into your body, which warms and melts away the hurt.

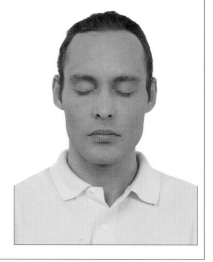

INNER VISION
Close your eyes and focus your thoughts, senses, and breathing. Use the power of visualization to fulfill your particular needs.

52 WHEN & WHERE TO VISUALIZE

You can use visualization in any circumstance where you feel the need to overcome negative feelings, apprehension, or to develop a more positive attitude. For example, it can be used to overcome stress in public situations. If you are in a crowded street and are feeling claustrophobic, visualize a clear space and sense of light surrounding your body: carry that feeling with you as you move around. If you feel vulnerable in the midst of strangers, visualize that you are encapsulated within a protective glass bell that shields you from harm.

YOU CAN FEEL SAFE & AT EASE EVEN IN A CROWD

HOW TO SLEEP WELL

53 WHY SLEEP IS IMPORTANT

Sleep is a natural healer. While you sleep, your metabolism slows down and you enter a state of deep relaxation. This gives your body time to recuperate from the day's physical activity, and it gives your brain the opportunity to process the information it received during the day. Your muscles relax and your endocrine system releases vital growth hormones, which promote the regeneration of cell tissues. The amount of sleep you need in order to feel refreshed varies according to each individual, but most adults require, on average, seven or eight hours per night.

Generally speaking, the older you get, the less sleep you need. Learn to value your sleep time and reap the benefits of improved mental clarity and physical vigor.

COMFORT & REST
A supportive mattress and pillow can aid sleep. Your bedroom should be well ventilated and should be neither too hot nor too cold.

TOO MANY LATE NIGHTS
The negative effects of too many late nights are numerous. You may have difficulty concentrating on work, make bad decisions, and become increasingly irritable and lethargic.

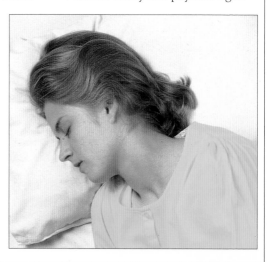

54 BALANCE WORK & LEISURE

A balance in your life between work and leisure improves your chances of a good night's sleep. If your work involves a high degree of responsibility, or if it is mentally stressful, counteract its negative demands with completely different activities in the evenings or at weekends. Socializing with close friends or enjoying physical exercise will help you to sleep.

△ GET PHYSICAL
Physical activity puts you back in touch with your body and helps you sleep.

◁ HAVE FUN
When your agenda is crowded, schedule time to meet friends outside work.

55 OVERCOMING LETHARGY

To overcome feelings of lethargy, establish a regular sleep pattern. Try to get up early so you will be healthily tired by bedtime, and be sure that you are in bed before midnight. During the day, take some brisk exercise in the fresh air and breathe deeply.

LOVE LIFE
Adopting good sleeping habits will help you rediscover your zest for life.

56 Organize your bedroom

Your bedroom should be a place of rest away from the activities of your busy life. To instill a sense of peace into your bedroom, keep it clean and uncluttered, and furnish it in soothing color tones (*Tip 94*). Organize the room so that you can store your clothing and personal effects. Treat it as your sanctuary, using the bedroom only for sleep, relaxation, and intimacy.

CUSTOM-MADE STORAGE

57 Bathing by candlelight

Soaking in a warm bath by the glow of candlelight is a perfect way to let the cares of the day wash away from you, preparing you for a restful night. Take a bath or shower at least an hour or two before your bedtime, and then relax and unwind by reading or listening to music.

AROMATIC BATH
Add a few drops of a relaxing aromatic essential oil such as sandalwood, chamomile, or lavender directly into the tub of water, and mix well before bathing.

58 HERBS TO UNWIND

Certain herbs act as safe and natural sedatives, helping you to relax and sleep. Many of these herbs can be infused in boiling water to make a tea, and some of them can be bought as mixtures in teabags. Either way, developing a taste for herbal teas provides you with sensible alternatives to caffeinated drinks. Sedative herbs include chamomile, lavender flower, vervain, and linden flower (lime).

59 COMPLETING THE DAY

Before retiring to bed, complete any unfinished business of the day: accomplish some simple tasks like tidying up your desk, the kitchen, or your bedroom. Make a list of what you need to do the next day. Then take time to relax so you can fall asleep with a clear mind.

PREPARE AHEAD
Get out clothes for the next day before you go to bed.

60 RELAXING OILS & CANDLES

Create a peaceful, soothing, and relaxing ambience in your bedroom by lighting candles and vaporizing soothing essential oils into the air with an aromatherapy burner. Rest and relax your whole body while breathing in the soporific fragrances. Candles are available specially scented with various essential oils. Take care to extinguish all your candles before falling asleep.

Put five drops of essential oil into bowl of water

SOOTHING AROMA
Aromatic essences such as lavender, chamomile, benzoin, neroli, cedarwood, jasmine, and rose are all sedatives.

61 Overcoming insomnia

Don't worry about the occasional episode of insomnia. Rather than fretting about sleep, it is better to rest comfortably in your bed and allow your body to relax. If your mind is overactive, make a warm non-alcoholic drink and read something light-hearted until you feel sleepy.

AVOID STRESS
Put aside anxious thoughts in the hours before sleep by making a decision to deal with pressing issues the next day.

62 Visualization to aid restful sleep

Close your eyes and imagine that your body is becoming heavier and more deeply relaxed with each exhalation of breath. Visualize that it is a warm, still night. You are lying in the soft, luxuriant grass of a meadow, bathed in the gentle glow of moonlight. With each cycle of breath, allow yourself to be filled with a deepening sense of peace.

LET GENTLE THOUGHTS EASE YOUR MIND

63 EASING INTO THE DAY

When you awaken in the morning, take time to savor the shift into consciousness by creating a positive frame of mind for the new day. Instead of leaping out of bed immediately and diving into frenetic activity, enjoy some tranquil moments recalling your dreams. If birds are singing, let them lull you into the day. Connect to your body by stretching out your limbs and your spine while you are still lying down. Exercise your facial muscles by making funny faces – pursing up your lips, and widening your eyes.

■ Avoid being jolted into the day by the sound of an alarm clock. Invest in an electric timer switch and wake up to the sound of gentle music on your CD, cassette, or radio.

■ Visualize a positive and creative day ahead of you, and think of all the good things that are yours to look forward to.

WAKING UP
Sit up in bed and stretch your arms out and above your head to expand your chest and lungs, then take in fresh oxygen by yawning deeply. Take five deep breaths.

GOOD NUTRITION

64 WHY EAT HEALTHILY?

Like all maxims, "you are what you eat" contains a great deal of truth. Research shows that a regular intake of certain foods reduces symptoms of aggression and anxiety, and helps to boost immunity to illness and disease. A nutritious, balanced diet increases vitality and is essential to your overall physical and mental well-being. Resolve to eat healthily so your diet can become a platform on which to build a relaxed and wholesome lifestyle.

65 WHAT IS A BALANCED DIET?

No single kind of food can supply all the nutritional requirements for optimum health. Aim to eat a balanced diet by choosing from a wide selection of foods that will provide the correct ratio of proteins, carbohydrates, fats, vitamins, and minerals that your body needs (*Tip 68*). Eat plenty of fibrous foods to aid the digestive process.

FRESH FOODS
A healthy and balanced diet will contain a large amount of fresh vegetables and fruit.

66 FOODS & DRINKS TO AVOID

However busy you are, do not allow yourself to become reliant on processed foods: these items are likely to be high in sugar and salt content and lacking in proper nutrients. Also, avoid refined foods, which have had vital nutrients removed. Choose whole-grain products where possible. Curb sugar intake to reduce the risk of obesity, tooth decay, and rapid changes in blood-sugar levels. Alcohol acts as a depressant and can cause mood swings; excessive intake is linked to serious diseases. Drink alcohol only in moderation.

AVOID CAFFEINE
Caffeine is a natural stimulant found in tea, coffee, cola drinks, and chocolate. Too much caffeine can cause anxiety, irritability, and heart palpitations.

REDUCE FATS
Cut down on rich, fatty foods, which will clog your arteries and impair your digestion.

67 PLAN YOUR SHOPPING

Take the stress out of food shopping by carefully planning ahead. Write down all your requirements for the week, and then keep to what is on your list. This will help you to resist impulse purchases and stay within your budget. Aim to shop regularly, so the food you eat is fresh.

OFF-PEAK SHOPPING
Try to shop at off-peak times when you will not be irritated by long lines. Don't shop when you are hungry: you're likely to buy junk food then.

BALANCE WEIGHT
Don't strain your muscles carrying heavy shopping bags. Balance the weight evenly in either hand.

68 PLANNING A NUTRITIOUS DIET

Choose wisely from the categories of foods shown here, and you can create a wide variety of tasty, low-fat, high-fiber meals that provide you with all the essential nutrients. Start the morning with a breakfast that contains protein, vitamins, and fiber, such as low-fat yogurt, cereal, and fruit. The bulk of your meals should be made up of complex carbohydrates, which will provide sufficient calories to meet your particular energy requirements. Eat fresh fruit or vegetables with every meal. Include protein in at least one meal a day to provide the amino acids your body needs.

PASTA

RICE

WHOLE-GRAIN BREAD

△ COMPLEX CARBOHYDRATES
Complex carbohydrates, such as whole-grain bread, cereals, pasta, whole-grain rice, and potatoes, provide fiber, calcium, iron, and B vitamins. Their calories create a healthier and more lasting energy source than sugar.

▽ VITAMINS & MINERALS
Fresh fruit and vegetables contain the essential vitamins, minerals, and trace elements that help your body to fight disease. Nuts and legumes provide an excellent source of protein, especially when combined with whole grains.

FRESH FRUIT

BRAZIL NUTS

KIDNEY BEANS

FRESH VEGETABLES

EGGS

CHICKEN

FISH

△ PROTEIN FOODS
Meat, fish, and eggs are the main sources of protein, iron, zinc, and B vitamins. Eat red meat and eggs sparingly since they are high in saturated fats.

YOGURT

SKIM MILK

REDUCED-FAT CHEESE

△ DAIRY PRODUCTS
Dairy products, such as yogurt, milk, and cheese, provide fats, vitamins, minerals, and protein. They are also important sources of calcium, which is vital for healthy teeth and bones. Low-fat varieties are best.

69 HEALTHY WAYS TO COOK

In preparing and cooking food, aim to conserve nutrients and minimize saturated fats. Store all perishables in the refrigerator at a temperature of 30–40°F (0–5°C) and discard stale items. Eat organic foods if possible, and use vegetable or olive oils rather than butter and other animal fats.

- Steam fresh vegetables to retain as many vitamins as possible.
- Broil, poach, or bake meat and fish to reduce fat content.
- Use water from boiled vegetables to make a nutritious soup stock.
- Choose lean cuts, and trim excess fat off meat.

STIR-FRY YOUR FOOD
Stir-frying vegetables in a wok is quick and easy and provides a tasty, appetizing, and nutritious meal.

70 EATING WITH AWARENESS

Food is more than simply sustenance. Mealtimes are occasions for celebration to be shared with friends and family. Turn meals into times for relaxation, preparing food with an appreciation of its nutritional value and its range of flavors. Present food so that it appeals to all the senses, and it will bring pleasure to your entire family.

FUN FOOD
Try to make mealtimes happy events.

71 AVOIDING THE AFTERNOON LOW

Blood-sugar levels can dip in the mid-afternoon, particularly after eating a heavy, high-carbohydrate lunch or after supplementing a meal with a sugary snack. This may lead to a drop in energy levels, causing lethargy, irritability, and poor concentration. A small snack – fresh fruit such as an orange, or raw vegetables with a slice of whole-grain bread – will provide a healthy pickup.

BRAIN FUELS
Eating fruit supplies a steady level of glucose into your bloodstream, which in turn fuels your brain.

72 DON'T EAT WHEN YOU ARE ANGRY

It is quite common for people to try to suppress feelings of anger and other uncomfortable emotions by turning to "comfort foods" – tasty but unwholesome snacks. Food eaten in this way is unlikely to be properly digested. Instead of eating, breathe deeply to relax your body. Then try to deal constructively with what is upsetting you.

73 GOOD DIGESTION

A relaxed state of mind and good digestion go hand in hand. Make time to sit down and eat moderately, thoroughly chewing each mouthful of food for better absorption. Cut down on refined and fatty foods, and eat plenty of fibrous foods such as whole-grain bread. Drink plenty of water and liquids during the day to aid digestion – certain herbal teas are excellent digestive aids.

DRINK FLUIDS
Drink lots of fresh water between meals to help your body absorb nutrients and eliminate toxins.

EAT REGULARLY
Have a good breakfast to help you avoid the temptation of snacking mid-morning. Eat three moderate-sized meals every day.

74 KICK THE HABIT

You may feel that smoking helps you to relax, but a cigarette is no real friend. Smoking is an addictive habit that causes serious health problems. It is not easy to quit smoking, but the benefits are immediate. Make up your mind to quit, and contact a doctor for advice if necessary.

BREAK THE HABIT
Acupuncture and hypnotherapy can help break bad habits.

LOOK AFTER YOUR LEISURE

75 PET THERAPY

Pets bring their owners great pleasure, in addition to being very therapeutic. Medical research has shown that the company of a pet calms nervous disorders, eases loneliness, and aids recovery of physical conditions. Stroking your cat or dog can help reduce high blood pressure, and walking your dog is an excellent form of daily exercise. Remember, however: keeping a pet is rewarding, but the responsibility is continuous.

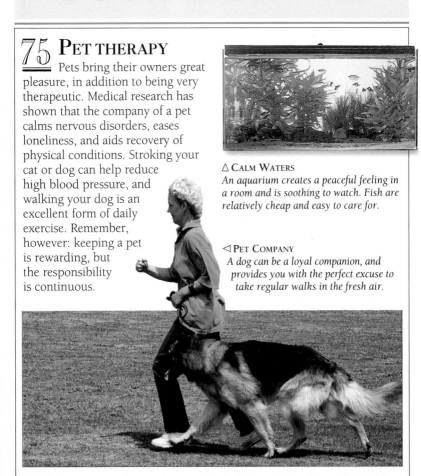

△ CALM WATERS
An aquarium creates a peaceful feeling in a room and is soothing to watch. Fish are relatively cheap and easy to care for.

◁ PET COMPANY
A dog can be a loyal companion, and provides you with the perfect excuse to take regular walks in the fresh air.

76 CULTIVATE A HOBBY

A hobby injects fresh interest into your life and encourages you to discover more about subjects that are unconnected to your routine. It can give you a sense of purpose when you spend time on your own, or it may provide you with opportunities to meet other people.

HOW DOES YOUR GARDEN GROW?
Gardening is a popular hobby. It expands your understanding of nature, keeps you active, and encourages creativity.

77 MUSICAL INTERLUDE

Music has a profound effect on mood, influencing the way you feel in any given moment. Soothing music is helpful in healing the body and calming the mind, while rhythmic music makes you feel more alert and alive. Listening to music is one of life's greatest pleasures. Ambient music, composed especially to aid relaxation, is becoming increasingly popular.

◁ **STRUM AWAY**
Learning to play a musical instrument is a rewarding pastime that focuses and stimulates the mind.

▷ **EASY LISTENING**
Develop an ear for music by listening to it in all its forms. Attend concerts and regularly tune in to music programs on the radio.

78 WALKING IN NATURE

Nature can return a sense of wholeness to your life. If you are mostly a city dweller, then take the occasional break and walk in the countryside so that you can escape the noise, traffic, and fumes of the city. Take time to absorb the beauty of nature again and to let your thoughts slow down. Being in the countryside will refresh and delight your senses with its scents, sights, and natural sounds. Simply walking in nature is a good tonic for body, mind, and spirit.

LEARN TO APPRECIATE THE NATURAL RHYTHM OF LIFE

79 ENJOY A SPORT

Many people would love to be more active and fit, but not everyone enjoys working out or going to a gym. If this kind of sport does not appeal to you, take up exercise that you can really enjoy. Let it become a fun part of your leisure life. Taking up a club sport, such as tennis or golf, can greatly enhance your social life.

PEDAL AWAY
Many sporting activities can be shared with friends as fun recreational pursuits.

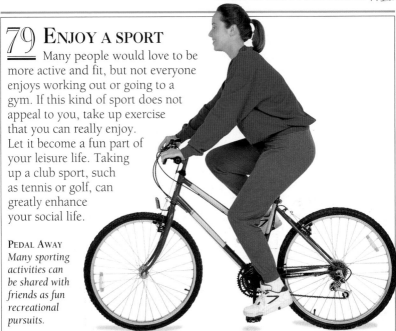

80 MAKE TIME FOR YOURSELF

Ensure that you take care of your own needs. If you are usually too busy looking after everyone else, each week make a realistic list of the things that you want to do for yourself, and aim to achieve them. Make space on your calendar for time to enjoy your own company.

GOOD READ
Create time to catch up on what you really enjoy.

81 EXPLORE YOUR CREATIVITY

Explore your unrecognized talents by devoting a portion of your leisure time to the expression of your creativity, so nurturing the artistic aspect of your nature. Practicing any form of art is therapeutic. The mental focus required by creative ventures counteracts the stresses encountered in your daily routine.

ARTISTIC SKILLS
Gain confidence in your creativity by participating in classes and workshops.

82 VACATIONS: GET AWAY FROM IT ALL

Vacations reconnect you with the more free-spirited and playful side of your nature, which can be dulled by the pressures of daily life. Even a weekend away provides a welcome break from tedious routines and hectic urban living. Longer vacations allow you to unwind completely, and enable you to tackle important issues with fresh vigor.

NEW PERSPECTIVE
Taking a break allows you to develop new perspectives and gives you time to assess what are your true priorities in life.

83 ADVANCE PLANNING

Plan your vacation times well in advance to ensure that you create quality time for relaxation in your busy schedule. This is particularly important if you are the principal breadwinner and are, therefore, more likely to forego impromptu breaks because of work pressure. Advance planning enables you to delegate work and to take care of domestic details, such as who will take care of pets. It encourages you to save for your vacation and to avoid the worry of bills on your return.

84 AWAY WITH YOUR PARTNER

Ensure a happy and relaxed vacation with your partner or with a friend by talking through your expectations of the vacation before leaving. People have very different ideas about how to enjoy leisure time, so understanding each other's wishes, and planning an itinerary in advance, will help to avert conflict. Agree to a budget that suits you both, and be prepared to compromise to get mutual satisfaction.

FLYING START
Get a vacation off to a good start by sharing vacation chores such as planning and booking travel, shopping for vacation items, and packing bags.

85 FAMILY VACATIONS

Plan family vacations so that everyone in the group, whatever their age or circumstance, has the opportunity to relax and enjoy themselves. Encouraging children to contribute toward planning the itinerary can help soothe sibling arguments. If you are a parent, choose vacation accommodation with reliable childcare services so that you can enjoy the occasional time alone with your partner.

HAVE FUN
A family vacation allows parents to get a well-earned rest and spend quality time with their children.

TAKE PRECAUTIONS
A comprehensive vacation insurance puts your mind at ease about the costs incurred by unfortunate mishaps. Take a first-aid kit for any minor health emergencies that arise.

86 PREPARING FOR A JOURNEY

Traveling to foreign countries is exciting, but it may be stressful. Culture shock and confusion can be reduced, however, if you equip yourself with knowledge of the customs and culture of your destination. Invest some time learning a few key words and simple phrases of the host country's language so you can communicate in a friendly manner with local people.

AVOID BOREDOM
Take along your favorite music tapes and a book to avoid boredom on a long-distance journey.

87 FLYING COMFORTABLY

Stay comfortable during long flights. Have a good night's sleep before embarking on the journey, and eat lightly before and during the flight. Avoid alcohol, since it increases dehydration, and drink lots of water. Exercise and stretch your limbs, even within the confines of your seat, to ease muscles and boost your circulation. If possible, take a walk in the fresh air as soon as you reach your destination.

◁ UPPER BODY
Clasp your fingers together and raise your arms. Roll your shoulders several times to stretch and release your neck.

◁ LOWER BODY
To reduce the risk of swollen feet, rotate your ankles in both directions and then press down onto the ball of your foot.

88 ON THE ROAD

Avoid becoming irritable, exhausted, or tense when driving long distances. Plan your journey so that you miss periods of traffic congestion on busy roads. Listen to music that will both soothe your nerves and keep you alert. Stop frequently, and get out of the car to stretch and breathe fresh air. Pack a flask of hot tea or coffee.

▷ EASE HANDS
Holding a steering wheel can cause tense wrists and hands. Try not to grip the wheel. Massage and flex your hands often (Tip 42).

▽ STIFF SHOULDERS
Frustration with traffic or prolonged sitting leads to stiff, hunched shoulders.

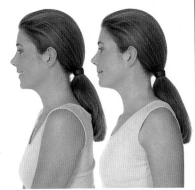

1 △ Curl your shoulders to stretch your back.

2 △ Pull your shoulders back to open your chest.

CREATE A RELAXING HOME

89 LIVING SIMPLY

Ideally, your home should be both a refuge from the turmoil and tensions of the outside world and a place of warmth and welcome. Aim for simplicity in your home, and you will soon notice how much more relaxing its atmosphere becomes. Try to make your rooms comfortable and visually relaxing. Once every month, go through your drawers and cupboards, and recycle items that you no longer use.

SIMPLICITY & CLEAN LINES ARE EASY ON THE EYE

90 CLEAR OUT CLUTTER

One of the greatest spatial stress factors in the home is the gradual accumulation of old bills, newspapers, correspondence, and junk mail. Valuable time can be wasted searching for one vital piece of written information. Organize your paperwork regularly, throwing out or recycling what you do not need and filing the rest away in an orderly fashion. Cut down on the amount of newspapers coming into your home, and toss junk mail.

BOX IT UP
Have clearly defined places to store each aspect of your paperwork. Filing boxes are handy, easy to obtain, and inexpensive.

91 MAKE YOUR OWN PRIVATE SPACE

Everyone benefits from having a certain amount of private space. Create a place in your home where you can retire – to think, read, write letters, or simply spend time on your own. If you do not have a separate study, utilize one corner of a room. Negotiate with your family or partner to make this your own personal area, and ask them not to disturb you while you are relaxing or attending to your own business.

PRIVATE SPACE
Your personal space should be a supportive environment in which you can accomplish your tasks in privacy and peace.

92 MAKE YOUR OWN MENTAL SPACE

Every so often, preferably once a week, create opportunities where you can reflect on your own personal issues and assimilate the changing thoughts and feelings that arise within you. Separate yourself from the demands of your loved ones, and take stock of your own needs. If it is hard to find a suitable space to be alone in your home, then retreat into the bathroom and lock the door behind you. Take a long bath and think things over. Ask your family to respect the fact that you want to spend some time on your own. Ensure that family members share the household tasks so you have time to yourself.

COMPASS
Feng shui, the Oriental art of placement, is becoming increasingly popular in the West. A feng shui expert uses a special compass to assess the energy flow in a house.

93 THE ART OF PLACEMENT

Your environment strongly influences your sense of well-being. Explore ways to make your immediate surroundings of home, garden, and office more harmonious. Hang mirrors strategically to increase the perception of light in a room, to reflect a pleasant view, or to create the illusion of extra space in confined areas. Wind chimes and mobiles create pleasant sounds and movement to help stimulate the atmosphere. Natural lighting brightens and cheers a room, and plants add life. Arrange furniture and other household items so that they do not cause dangerous obstructions or unsightly lines.

FENG SHUI
According to the ancient Chinese system of feng shui, your surroundings should be in harmony with the flow of universal life energy, called ch'i, to encourage prosperity and health in your life.

94 CHOOSING & USING COLORS

Color influences your moods and is an essential factor when you are deciding on how to decorate and furnish your rooms. Certain hues stimulate or relax; others inspire or soothe. Color should aid your functions and needs within a particular space. Try new color combinations to break away from tried and tested formulas, and so create a fresh sense of adventure in your home. Using no more than three or four colors in one area, select subtly varying shades of monochromatic, harmonious blends of closely related colors, or bright and vivacious contrasts of opposing colors.

BLUES
Blue is a soothing color. It is said to aid creativity and communication.

REDS
Warm and vibrant, red is a stimulating color that is associated with energy.

WHITES
White embraces the whole spectrum. Its neutral tone imparts clarity and purity.

YELLOWS
A stimulating color, yellow brings the cheering feel of sunshine to a room.

GREENS
Uplifting yet relaxing, green is associated with nature and feelings of love.

ORANGES
Orange brings warm earth tones into a home, creating a sense of stability.

95 USING NATURAL MATERIALS

Sleeping between freshly laundered cotton sheets always feels wonderfully relaxing. Clothes made from natural materials are a more healthy choice to have close to your body than synthetic fibers. Natural fabrics allow your skin to breathe easily and your vital energy to flow more freely. Change into loose-fitting, natural-fiber clothing to feel really comfortable when you get home after a hard day's work.

FRESH LINEN
Natural materials look and feel good. Keep your linen cupboard fresh and scented by using muslin bags filled with lavender.

96 WARMTH & VENTILATION

Avoid overheating your home, and ensure that it is well ventilated at all times. Maintaining the correct balance between warmth and ventilation will help you to feel relaxed and at ease, and also alert and energetic. Central heating, while creating uniform warmth, dries the atmosphere, which may affect your health and skin. Buy a humidifier to replace lost moisture, or place small containers of water close to the radiators.

FRESH AIR
Open the windows in your home daily to let in fresh air and let out stale smells so that you remain fresh and alert.

97 LET IN LIGHT

Natural light has a positive influence on your health and mood; lack of it can lead to lethargy and depression. Artificial lighting may cause headaches, low energy, and eye strain. Try to bring as much natural lighting as possible into your home. If window position or neighboring buildings allow little light, place mirrors strategically to reflect what light there is, or buy special electric bulbs that simulate natural light. Place them particularly in areas of activity to enhance energy and concentration.

BRIGHTEN UP
Let as much natural light as possible into your home and everything, including you, will brighten up as a result.

98 SOFT LIGHTING

During the evening, relax in the glow of soft lighting. Place low-wattage lamps or lighted candles in areas that best complement the cast of their light. Soft lighting makes it easier to rest and creates a gentle, more intimate ambience in a room when you have guests. Use scented candles to enhance the atmosphere of relaxation, but be sure to snuff them out before you go to sleep.

BEDROOM GLOW
Keep the lights low in your bedroom so that it conveys a sleepy feeling and becomes your haven of rest. Choose fine curtains so that the early morning light awakens you and revives your spirits.

99 PEACE & QUIET

Once in a while, put a stop on activity. Turn off all forms of stimulation in your home, such as the television, radio, or the stereo system, and unplug your telephone. Allow peace and quiet to descend on your surroundings and just sit quietly, doing nothing. Close your eyes and simply be aware of your breathing and the stillness of the moment. Let your whole awareness be absorbed into the present moment of being.

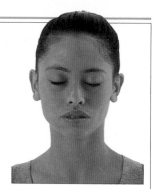

RELAX YOUR MIND

100 BRING NATURE INDOORS

Houseplants enhance the beauty and tranquility of your home. They bring a breath of nature into your living environment – which is particularly important if you don't have a garden. Select plants for their ability to thrive indoors, and also consider their shape, color, and fragrance. Avoid toxic plants if you have children or pets. Place plants where they add softer contours to the straight angles of a room. Green and silver foliage are relaxing, while reds and purples stimulate.

SUNLIGHT
Position your plants carefully according to the amount of natural light they require.

CONTAINER-GROWN HERBS
Keep herbs in pots in your kitchen. Use their fragrant leaves in cooking to benefit from their therapeutic properties.

101 AN OUTDOOR RETREAT

If you are fortunate enough to have a garden, let it become the perfect retreat for you. Make it a haven where you can spend quiet time in solitude or relax in the company of friends. Creating features such as a fountain or pond, or hanging wind chimes, adds to the soothing atmosphere. Encourage wildlife to your garden by hanging birdfeeders in areas that are safe from cats, and grow plants that attract butterflies.

FLOWER POWER
Few things bring greater joy than a display of blooms from plants that you have carefully tended. Cultivate fragrant varieties to delight your nose as well.

INDEX

Acknowledgments

Dorling Kindersley would like to thank Hilary Bird for compiling the index; Richard Hammond for proofreading; Alice Butler MB, Ch.B. for consultancy; Robert Campbell and Mark Bracey for DTP assistance; Marianna Sonnenberg for picture research; Karen Fielding for makeup and hair; and Ralf Beck, Lucie de Keller, and Julian Ormerod for modeling.

Photography
KEY: t *top*; b *bottom*; c *center*; l *left*; r *right*
Robert Harding 46b, 52t, 66bl; Imagebank 23br, 52t, 58bl;
Leon Krier 63bl; Photographer's Library 41b, 58b;
Superstock 23bl, 55br, 60cr